Inside My Body

Why Do I Need Glasses?

Carol Ballard

Raintree
Chicago, Illinois

www.heinemannraintree.com
Visit our website to find out
more information about
Heinemann-Raintree books.

To order:
☎ Phone 888-454-2279
▣ Visit www.heinemannraintree.com
to browse our catalog and order online.

Edited by Kate de Villiers and Vaarunika Dharmapala
Designed by Steve Mead
Illustrations by KJA-artists.com
Picture research by Mica Brancic

Originated by Capstone Global Library Ltd
Printed in the United States of America by Worzalla
Publishing

15 14 13 12 11 10
10 9 8 7 6 5 4 3 2 1

Library of Congress Cataloging-in-Publication Data
Ballard, Carol.
  Why do I need glasses? : vision / Carol Ballard.
    p. cm. — (Inside my body)
  Includes bibliographical references and index.
  ISBN 978-1-4109-4010-0 (hc) — ISBN 978-1-4109-
4021-6 (pb) 1. Vision—Juvenile literature. 2. Vision
disorders—Juvenile literature. 3. Eyeglasses—Juvenile
literature. 4. Eye—Juvenile literature. I. Title. II. Title:
Vision.
  QP475.7.B364 2011
  612.8'4—dc22   2010024671

Acknowledgments
The author and publisher are grateful to the following
for permission to reproduce copyright material: Alamy
pp. **12** (© Stuwdamdorp), **16** (© Natural Visions/Heather
Angel), **21** (© Phil Degginger), **24** (© Bob Daemmrich);
Corbis p. **11** (© Visuals Unlimited); Getty Images
pp. **4** (Comstock Images/Jupiterimages), **13** (National
Geographic/Beverly Joubert), **18** (Blend Images/Ned
Frisk), **27** (Blend Images/Ronnie Kaufman); Science
Photo Library pp. **9** (Ralph Eagle), **14** (Omikron), **15**
(David Nicholls), **17** (Power and Syred), **19** (Steve Allen),
25 (Will & Deni McIntyre); Shutterstock pp. **5** (Bruce
MacQueen), **6** (RTimages), **10**, **22**, **23**, **29 butterfly**
(© Sofia), **20**, **23**, **27 band aid** (© Isaac Marzioli), **20**,
23, **27 gauze** (© Yurok).

Cover photograph of a boy wearing glasses reproduced
with permission of Getty Images (Comstock Images).

We would like to thank David Wright for his invaluable
help in the preparation of this book.

Every effort has been made to contact copyright holders
of material reproduced in this book. Any omissions will
be rectified in subsequent printings if notice is given to
the publisher.

Contents

Words that appear in the text in bold, **like this**, are explained in the glossary on page 30.

Seeing the World

You use your eyes to find out about the world around you. You are able to see huge things such as mountains and oceans, and tiny things such as beetles and grains of sand. You can detect movement and color, as well as judge distances and positions—all thanks to your eyes.

A sense of sight

Your sense of sight is very important. Imagine trying to eat your dinner if you could not see the plate or the food on it. Imagine dressing or brushing your hair without sight.

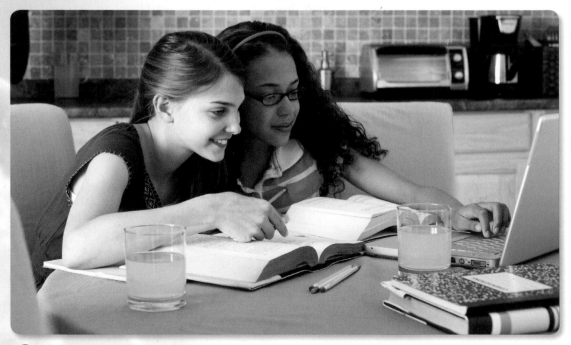

Some people, such as the girl on the right, cannot see clearly. They must wear glasses to help them.

Your eyes keep you safe. Without your sight, walking along a sidewalk or crossing a street would be difficult and dangerous.

Your sense of sight can also help to entertain you. How would you watch television or read a book if you could not see? Sports such as soccer and tennis would be impossible if you could not see the ball or the other players.

Have you ever looked closely at your eyes, or thought about how they work? Why do some people need to wear glasses, but others do not?

This red-tailed hawk has sharper eyesight than any other animal.

Extreme body fact

The sharpest eyesight
A red-tailed hawk's eyesight is about eight times sharper than that of humans. This bird can spot a mouse on the ground from 1.6 kilometers (1 mile) away! A human with average eyesight would have to be closer than 200 meters (220 yards) to see the mouse.

What Is Around My Eyes?

You have one eye on each side of your nose. The parts of your face around your eyes help to keep them clean.

Above each eye is a ridge of skin covered by a line of hairs. These are called eyebrows. They help to stop dust and sweat from getting in your eyes. Around the eyes are loose flaps of skin called eyelids. Along the edge of each eyelid is another line of hairs called eyelashes. Eyelashes prevent dust and dirt from getting into your eyes.

Here you can see a pair of eyes with eyebrows, eyelids, and eyelashes.

Blinking helps to keep your eyes moist and clean. When you blink, your upper eyelid moves quickly down to meet your bottom eyelid. Blinking sweeps a thin layer of fluid across the eye. This cleans the eye and keeps it moist.

What happens when I cry?

Tears are the fluid that keep your eyes clean. They are made high up under your upper eyelids. They travel to your eyes through tiny tubes. Tears will usually drain away through more tubes, from your eyes to your nose.

When you cry, the tears flow so quickly that they cannot all drain away. Some spill out of your eyes and down your face. You might cry for many different reasons. You might cry because you are happy or sad, because you have hurt yourself or have been laughing a lot, or even when you yawn!

SCIENCE BEHIND THE MYTH

MYTH: Cutting onions makes you cry.

SCIENCE: It's true! Onions contain a substance that irritates your eyes and makes your eyes water, often while you are chopping them. You can solve the problem by chilling the onion before you cut it or by holding it under water while you cut it.

What Is Inside My Eyes?

You can see only a small part of each eye. Most of your eye is hidden and protected by the bones of your face. Each eye is round like a ball and is often called an eyeball.

The bony ring around each eye is called an eye socket. Six muscles hold the eyeball in place in the socket. These muscles control your eye movements.

sclera

retina

cornea

iris

watery liquid

pupil

optic nerve

lens

jelly-like fluid

🔍 This diagram shows you some of the parts of an eye.

The front of the eye

The whole eyeball is covered by a tough outer layer called the **sclera**. The part of the sclera that you can see at the front of the eye is the **cornea**. The cornea is see-through. It allows light to pass into the eye.

Behind the cornea is a colored ring of muscle called the **iris**. In the middle of this is the **pupil**. This looks like a black circle, but it is really a hole that lets light into the inside of the eye. The iris controls the size of the pupil.

Behind the pupil is a jelly-like disc called the **lens**. This is held in place by tiny muscles that control its shape. The space between the cornea and lens is filled with watery liquid.

This is a photograph of a real eye. Compare it to the diagram on page 8. Can you find the cornea, pupil, iris, and lens?

The back of the eye

The space inside the eyeball behind the lens is filled with a soft jelly. The inside of the eyeball is covered with a thin layer called the **retina**. The retina is linked to the **optic nerve**, and the optic nerve is linked to the brain.

How Do My Eyes Work?

Did you know that an eye is like a camera? Cameras and eyes both have a hole for light to enter and a **lens** to bend the light. They can both capture an **image**.

Light travels in straight lines from a light source, such as the Sun or a lightbulb. When it hits something, it bounces off in every direction. If some of the light enters your eye, you will be able to see the object.

light rays are first bent by the cornea

an upside-down image forms on the retina

light rays are also bent by the lens

a message goes from the optic nerve to the brain

🔍 This diagram shows how an image is formed at the back of the eye.

How does my eye use light to help me see?

1. Light bounces off an object to your eye.

2. Light passes through the **cornea**, which bends the light a little.

3. Light passes through the lens, which bends it even more. This is important, because if the light is bent too much, or not enough, you will see only a blurry image.

4. Light travels to the back of the eye. It makes an upside-down image of the object on the **retina**.

5. The retina reacts when the light hits it and sends a message to the **optic nerve**.

6. The optic nerve carries the message to the brain.

7. The brain makes sense of the message, and you see the object.

Extreme body fact

Squid eyes
This Southern squid has very good eyesight. Other types of squid have huge eyes, which can be even bigger than your head!

Why Can't I see in the Dark?

Look at your eyes in a mirror. How big is the **pupil**? Now shut your eyes for a couple of minutes. Look again. Does your pupil look bigger?

Bright light

In bright light, the **iris** makes the pupil smaller. This lets less light enter the eye. It helps to protect the eye from very bright light that might damage it.

🔍 In dim light (left), the pupil is large to let as much light as possible enter the eye. In bright light (right), the pupil is small to stop too much light from entering the eye.

Some animals, such as this leopard, have an extra layer behind the retina. This reflects light back into the eye. When a light shines onto the eye, the pupil seems to glow from this reflected light.

Dim light

In dim light, the iris makes the pupil bigger. This lets more light enter the eye. It helps you to see even when the light is very dim.

Your eyes do need some light to work. When it is completely dark, and there is no light at all, you cannot see anything.

SCIENCE BEHIND THE MYTH

MYTH: Eating carrots helps you to see in the dark.

SCIENCE: Yes, but only in some cases. The **retina** needs vitamin A to work in dim light. If at some point you are short of vitamin A, eating carrots can help. But if you already have enough vitamin A, eating carrots will not help you see any better at all!

How Do I See Colors?

We can see all the colors of the rainbow. Do you know how? The **retina** plays a key part in how we see color. It is made up of two types of very tiny building blocks called **rods** and **cones**. Rods are long and thin. Cones are short and fat.

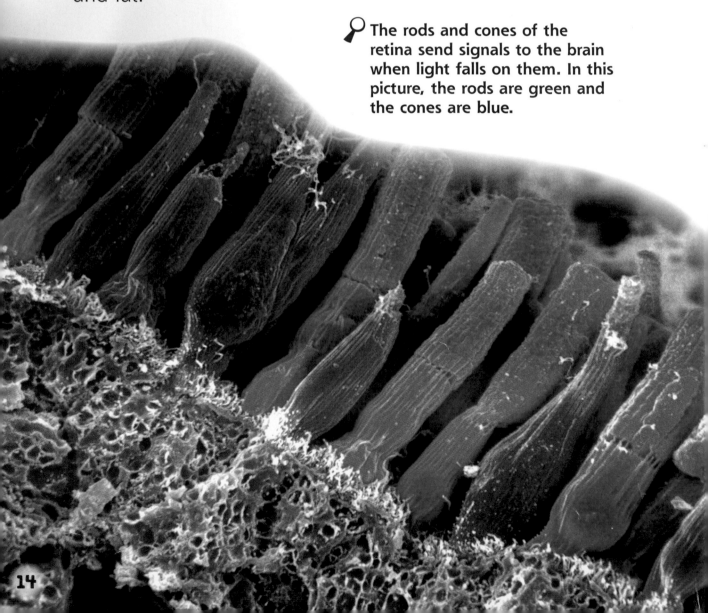

The rods and cones of the retina send signals to the brain when light falls on them. In this picture, the rods are green and the cones are blue.

Rods and cones

Rods cannot detect the color of light. They react to all light in the same way. Without cones, you would see everything as black, gray, and white.

There are three different types of cone. One detects red light, another detects green light, and the third detects blue light. If you look at something red, only red cones respond. If you look at something blue, only blue cones respond. If you look at something purple, some red cones and some blue cones will respond.

The brain figures out the color you are looking at from the numbers of red, blue, and green cones that respond.

Color blindness

Some people cannot see the full range of colors that most people do. Some of their cones do not work properly. These people are said to be **color blind**. The most common type of color blindness is when red and green things look like exactly the same color.

This is a color blindness test card. To a person with red-green color blindness, all the dots would appear to be the same color.

Why Do I Have Two Eyes?

Hold one finger out in front of you. Shut one eye and look at it. Now quickly shut that eye and open the other one. Does it look as if your finger has jumped?

This happens because each eye gets a slightly different view of your finger. When your brain receives the signals from each eye, it puts them together. It combines the information to figure out exactly where your finger is.

In humans, both eyes move together. Chameleons can move each eye separately. They can look in two different directions at the same time!

Distance, speed, and direction

Having two eyes helps you to judge distance, speed, and direction. This is really important for pouring juice into a glass, catching a ball, or stepping off a curb. It is even more important for people such as pilots, surgeons, and drivers. These people have to be able to judge distances, speed, and directions very accurately in their work.

Compound eyes

Insects such as fruit flies have compound eyes. This means that their eyes are made up of hundreds of tiny **lenses**. Each takes a tiny snapshot view. These **images** are then put together to make up a single complete picture. This is similar to a computer screen or television screen, where pictures are made up from patterns of tiny dots.

In this enlarged photograph, you can see the many lenses that make up a fruit fly's eye. Hairs on the lenses help to keep them clean.

What Does an Optometrist Do?

Optometrists test eyes. Their results tell them how well a person can see and, if needed, they can give **lenses** to help the patient see better. Their results also help them tell whether the patient's eyes are healthy.

Testing sight

One test that optometrists use is a chart with letters on it. The letters at the top are bigger than the letters at the bottom. The optometrist asks the person to read down the chart. The better the person's eyesight, the further down he or she will be able to read.

$\mathcal{P}$ **Here an optometrist is looking inside a boy's eyes to check that everything is alright.**

Testing health

Another test that optometrists use is to shoot a puff of air at the front of the eyeball. This helps to measure the pressure inside the eyeball. The pressure reading tells the optometrist whether the person's eye is healthy or not.

Optometrists also test eyes by shining lights into them so they can see the **retina** at the back. They look to see whether the retina is healthy or damaged.

Some optometrists use a dome in which lights flash randomly one at a time over the inside of the dome. The person clicks a button each time he or she sees a light. This tells the optometrist whether the person can see equally well in all directions.

This is a photograph of a human retina. The fine red lines are blood vessels that carry blood through the retina to keep it healthy and working properly.

Why Do I Need Glasses?

Do you wear glasses? Lots of people need glasses, and chances are that either you or some of your friends or family do. Do you know why some people need to wear glasses?

Some people can see everything around them clearly. However, many other people do not have perfect vision. They wear glasses to help them see better.

Practical advice

Wearing glasses

If you have glasses, remember to follow your **optometrist's** instructions about when you should wear them. Keep them in their case when you are not wearing them. Before you put them on, clean them with a soft cloth to remove dust and smudges. Visit your optometrist regularly.

Seeing clearly

Some people can clearly see things that are near to them, but far away things look blurred. This is called being **nearsighted**. Some people have the opposite problem: they can clearly see far away things, but things close to them are blurred. This is called being **farsighted**.

Some people see things as bent or twisted. Others see everything double. Wearing glasses can help with all of these problems.

A farsighted person might see these clearly:
- a person standing far away
- the picture on a television screen
- the view from a window.

A nearsighted person might see these as a blur.

A nearsighted person might see these clearly:
- a person standing nearby
- their dinner plate
- a package they pick up from the supermarket shelf.

A farsighted person might see these as a blur.

How Do My Glasses Help Me See?

If an **optometrist** thinks you need help with your eyesight, he or she may suggest that you wear glasses. Different types of eye problems need different types of glasses. The **lenses** in the glasses bend the light to help you see clearly.

Being nearsighted

People who are **nearsighted** cannot see things in the distance clearly. The light entering the eye is bent too much, so it does not strike the **retina** correctly. This makes a fuzzy **image**. They need glasses with lenses that bend the light to make it strike the retina corrrectly and make a clear image.

a blurred image forms on the retina

light rays are bent outward by the lens

light rays from a distant object

concave lens

a clear image forms on the retina

🔍 Here you can see a nearsighted eye and a lens that corrects the problem.

Being farsighted

People who are **farsighted** cannot see things close to them. Their eyes do not bend the light enough, and the light entering the eye does not strike the retina correctly. This makes a fuzzy image. They need glasses with lenses that bend the light to make it strike the retina correctly and make a clear image.

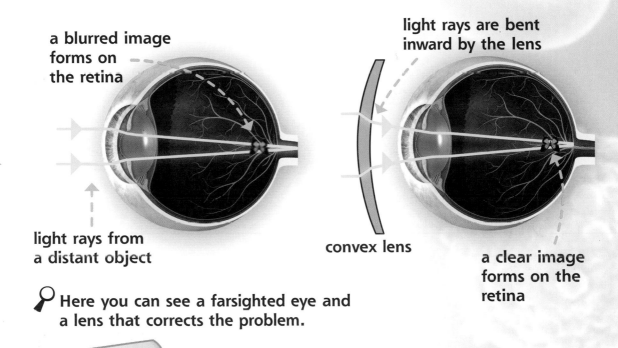

a blurred image forms on the retina

light rays from a distant object

light rays are bent inward by the lens

convex lens

a clear image forms on the retina

Here you can see a farsighted eye and a lens that corrects the problem.

Practical advice

I hate my glasses!

If you hate wearing glasses, contact lenses may be for you. Contact lenses are tiny discs that sit on the front of the eye. These bend light just as glasses do. However, contact lenses are not right for everybody. Your optometrist will tell you whether you can wear them.

What It I Am Blind?

Many people are blind. Some blind people can see nothing at all. Others may be able to see some shadowy, blurred **images** or be able to detect some movements around them.

Being blind can make everyday things, such as reading a book or watching television, very difficult or even impossible. However, modern technology can help many blind people to overcome their disability.

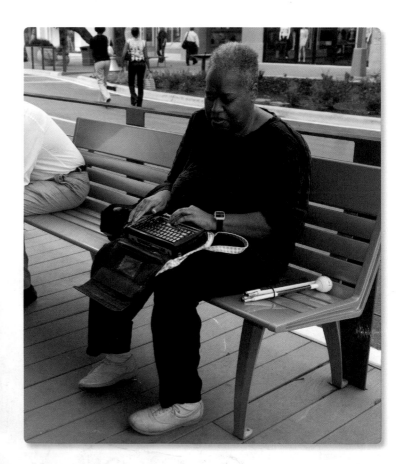

Blind people can use computers that have been made specially for them.

Braille

One of the earliest aids for blind people was the Braille alphabet. This uses a different pattern of dots for each letter and number. Blind people feel the dots with their fingers to reads the letters or numbers.

Getting around

Guide dogs can be trained to help blind people to get around safely. GPS (Global Positioning System) can also be used. GPS receivers, which can be worn or held, figure out exactly where a person is. These receivers can give blind people directions to where they want to go to and help them to avoid obstacles in their paths.

A blind person can enjoy reading an exciting story that is written in Braille.

How Can I Take Care of My Eyes?

Your eyes are very important. They are also very delicate. Here are some tips to help you take care of your eyes:

- Keep your eyes clean by washing your face at least twice a day.

- Wear ski goggles to protect your eyes from glare if you are out in the snow.

- Wear sunglasses to protect your eyes from bright sunshine on a sunny day.

- NEVER look directly at the Sun or at an eclipse. The light is so bright it can permanently damage your eyes.

- Wear eye protection for sports.

- If your **optometrist** prescribes glasses for you, make sure you follow his or her instructions about wearing them.

- If you wear contact **lenses**, follow all the instructions, such as how long you can wear them for, when to change them for new ones, and how to clean them.

🔍 Taking care of your eyes will help them stay healthy, so you can see and enjoy the world around you.

Something in your eye?

If something is in your eye, do not rub it. This will make it feel worse. Instead, splash it with plenty of water to flush away whatever was causing the problem. If this does not work, you might need to see a doctor or nurse.

Alert! If you splash any chemicals in your eye, try to flush the eye clean with water and seek medical help quickly.

All About Eyes

Each person has **irises** that are different from anybody else's. This means irises can be used to identify someone, just like fingerprints.

Did you know that you blink 10 to 15 times a minute? That is more than 10,000 blinks a day. Babies blink only about twice a minute.

Wearing colored contact **lenses** can make you look very different. There are all sorts of colors available, from normal eye colors such as blue and brown, to amazing shades of red and yellow. Some are even patterned with flames or fur!

Unlike most parts of your body, your eyes hardly grow at all. By the time you are an adult, they will be only a few millimeters bigger than when you were born!

Parts of the eye

sclera

cornea

pupil

iris

lens

image on retina

retina

muscle

optic nerve

Glossary

blood vessel tube through which blood travels around the body

color blind inability to tell some colors apart

cone part of the retina that allows you to see colors

cornea see-through layer at the front of the eye

farsighted to be able to see distant objects clearly, but close objects less clearly

image picture of something

iris colored ring of muscle around the pupil

lens jelly-like disc in the eye that bends light

nearsighted to be able to see close objects clearly, but distant objects less clearly

optic nerve part that carries messages from the retina to the brain

optometrist person who tests eyes and prescribes glasses

pupil hole at the front of the eye that lets light enter the eye

retina thin layer inside the eyeball that reacts to light

rod part of the retina that allows you to see light

sclera tough, white wall that keeps the eye in a ball shape

Find Out More

Books

Ballard, Carol. *Understanding the Senses (Understanding the Human Body)*. New York: Rosen, 2010.

Bender, Lionel. *Explaining Blindness (Explaining)*. Mankato, Minn.: Smart Apple Media, 2010.

Stewart, Melissa. *The Eyes Have It: The Secrets of Eyes and Seeing*. New York: Marshall Cavendish Benchmark, 2010.

Websites

http://kidshealth.org/kid/htbw/eyes.html
Discover more about eyes at this website.

http://faculty.washington.edu/chudler/chvision.html
Find several fun vision experiments at this website.

www.nfb.org/nfb/nopbc_questions_kids_ask.asp
This website offers answers to questions kids commonly ask about blindness.

Index